Dear Parent,

In <u>What Is a Mountain?</u> your child will
learn how mountains are formed. Big
Bear draws pictures of the many layers
of different kinds of rocks found in
mountains for Christopher and his
friends. Then he takes them on a climb
up a mountain to meet some animals
that live there. Are you ready to go
mountain climbing? Bring along a
strong rope and remember to stay close
together as you begin your mountain
adventure.

Sincerely,

Rita D. Gould

Managing Editor

FAMILY FUN

- Using a world atlas, help your child to
  locate the following mountains and
  mountain ranges:
  North America—Mount McKinley,
  Mount St. Helens, Rocky Mountains
  Europe—Matterhorn, Etna
  Asia—Mount Everest, Fuji
  Africa—Mount Kilimanjaro

READ MORE ABOUT IT

- *What Is a Volcano?*
- *What Is an Ocean?*

WEEKLY READER BOOKS presents

What Is a Mountain?

A **Just Ask**™ Book

Hi, my name is Christopher!

by Chris Arvetis
and Carole Palmer

illustrated by
Terry Rose

FIELD PUBLICATIONS
MIDDLETOWN, CT.

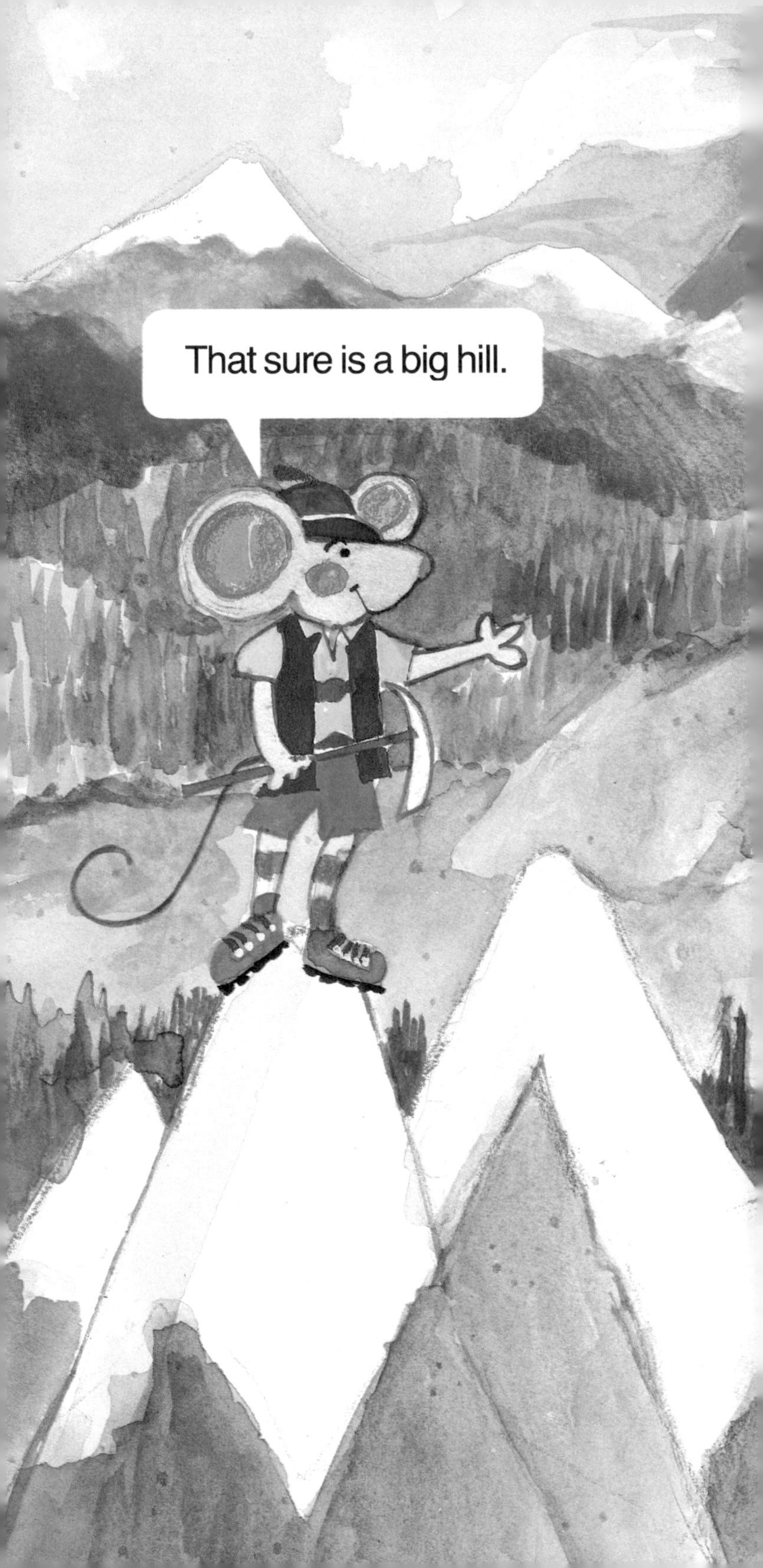
That sure is a big hill.

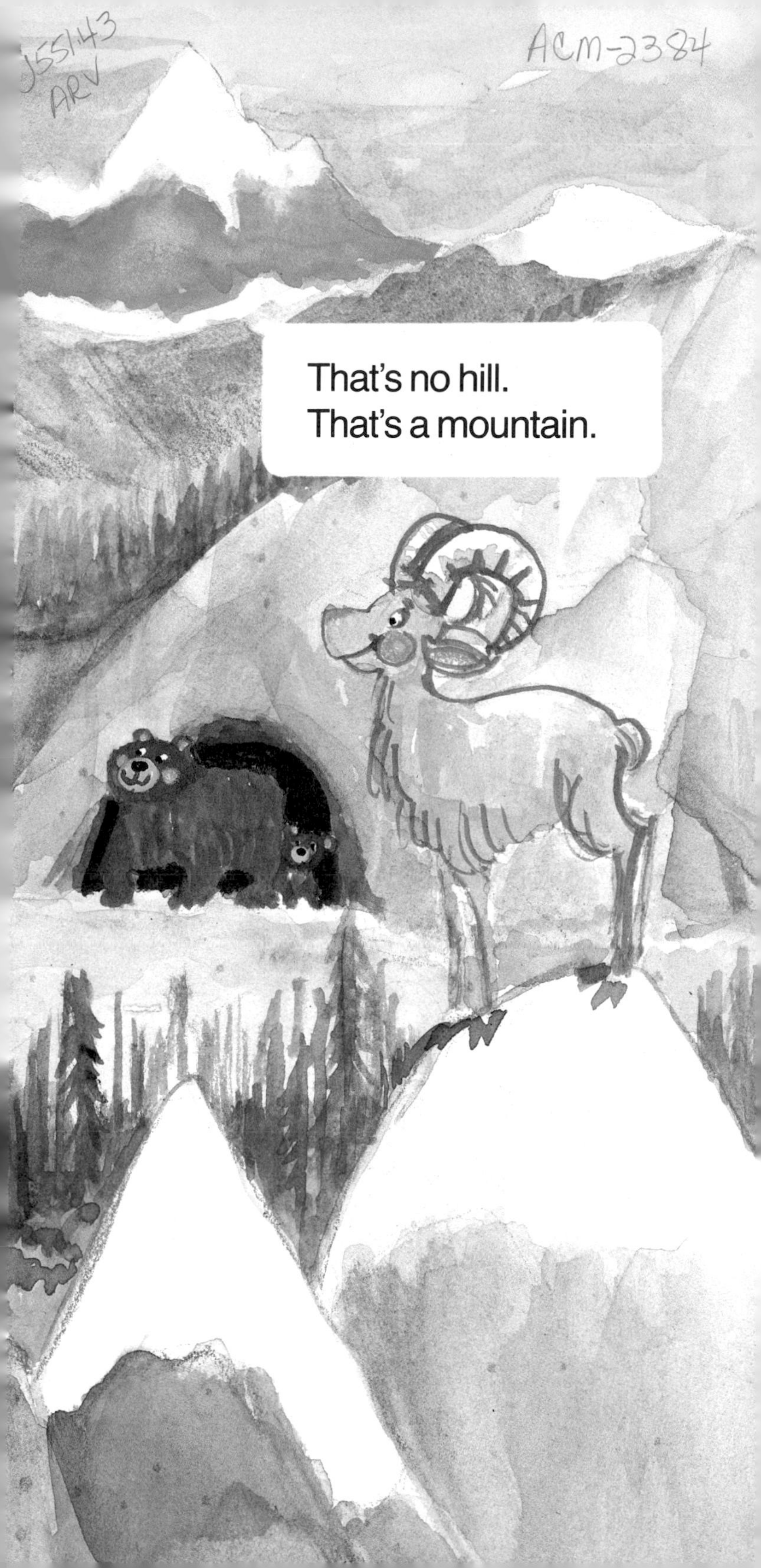
That's no hill.
That's a mountain.

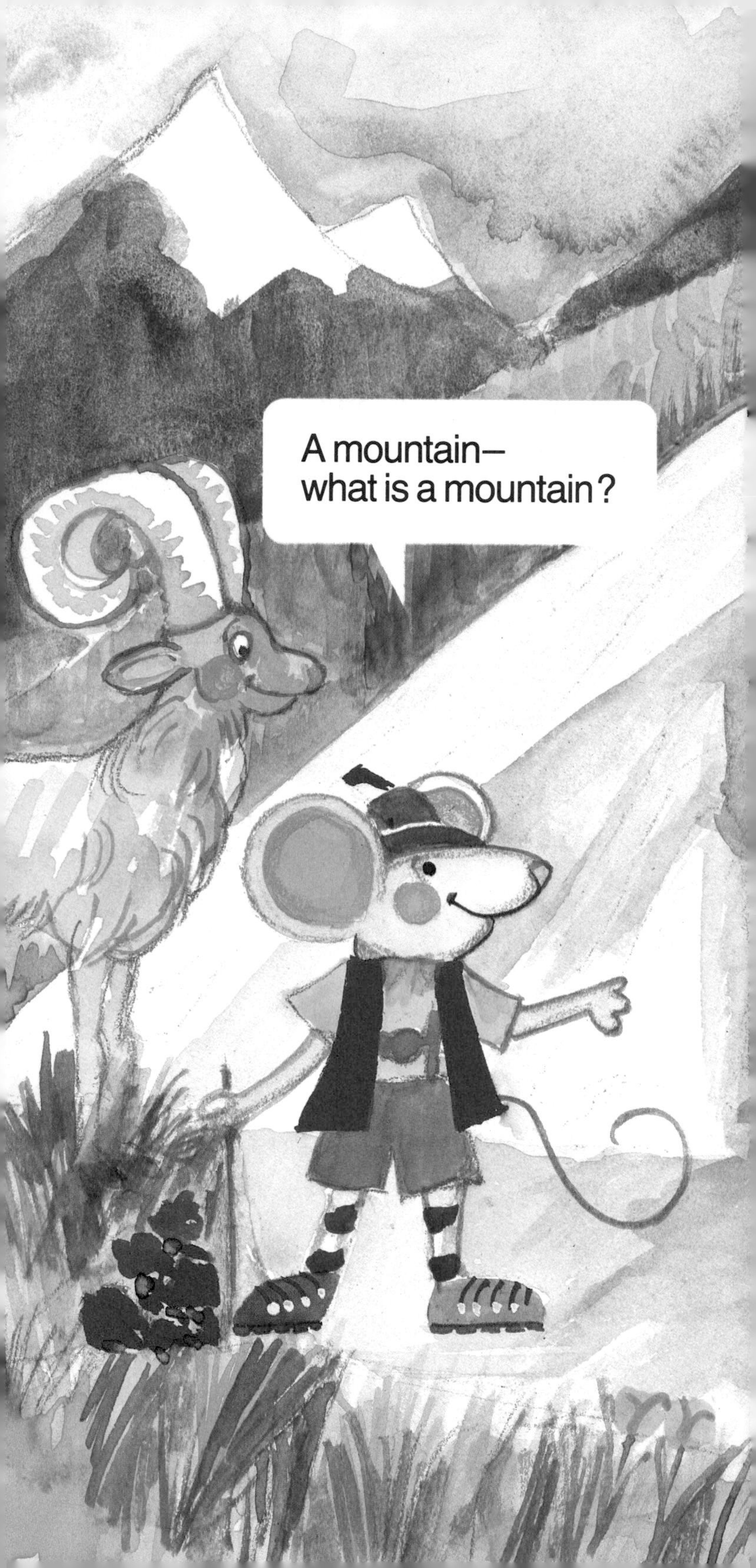
A mountain–
what is a mountain?

A mountain is part of the earth that is much higher than the land around it. Mountains have long slopes and high tops.

Mountains were created
a long, long time ago.
Mountains were made
in several ways.
Let me show you how
some were formed.

Long, long ago, movement in the earth squeezed layers of rock into folds that look like curves.

In some places the rocks were not folded a lot.
These places stayed raised and flat.
They are called plateaus.
Let's say that together—
PLA-TEAUS.

PLA-TEAUS!

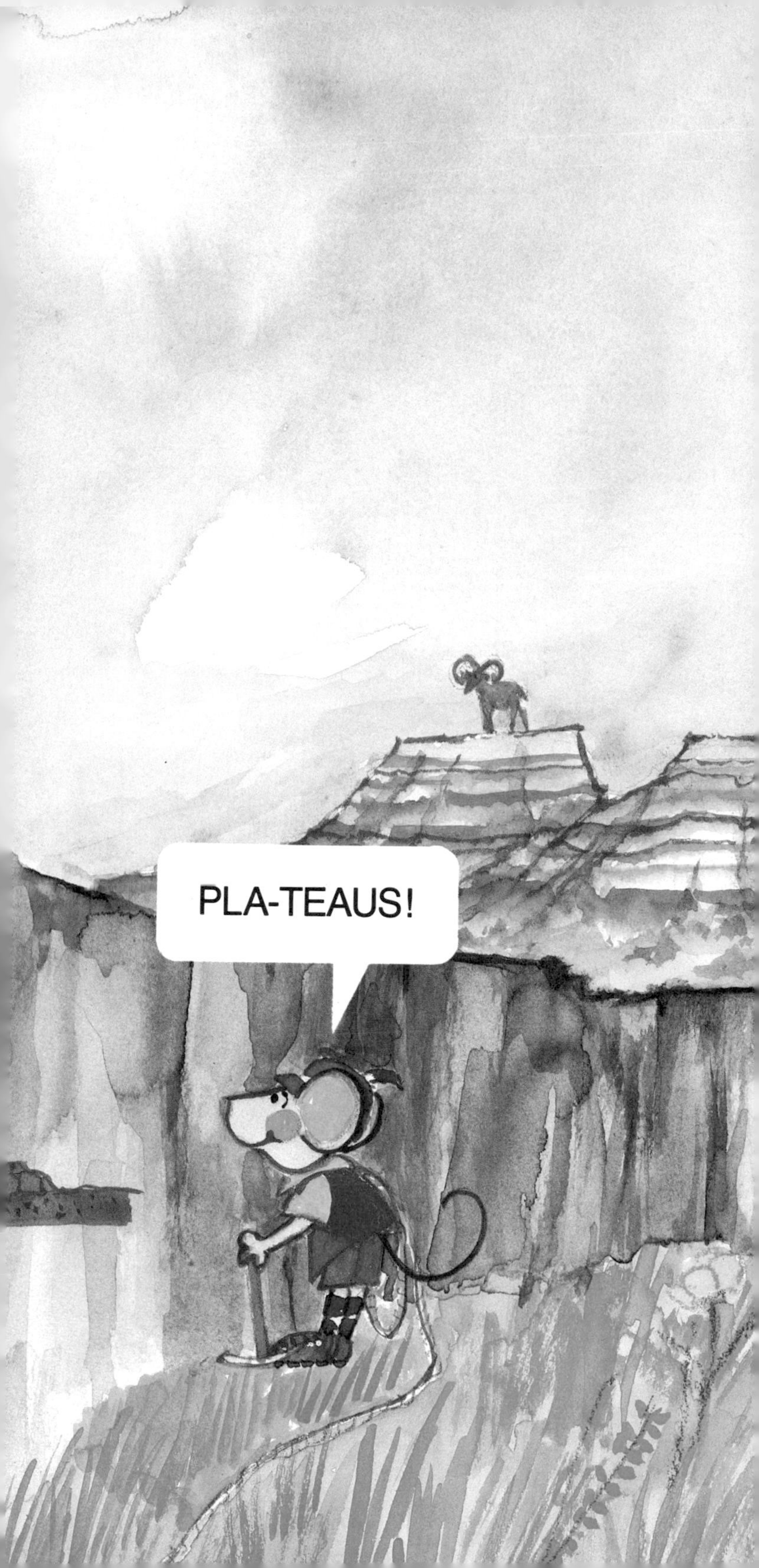
PLA-TEAUS!

Some land around the plateaus was washed away by the wind and the water.
Hilly land was left.
These hills look like tabletops and are called mesas.

Another kind of mountain was made when rocks broke into huge blocks.

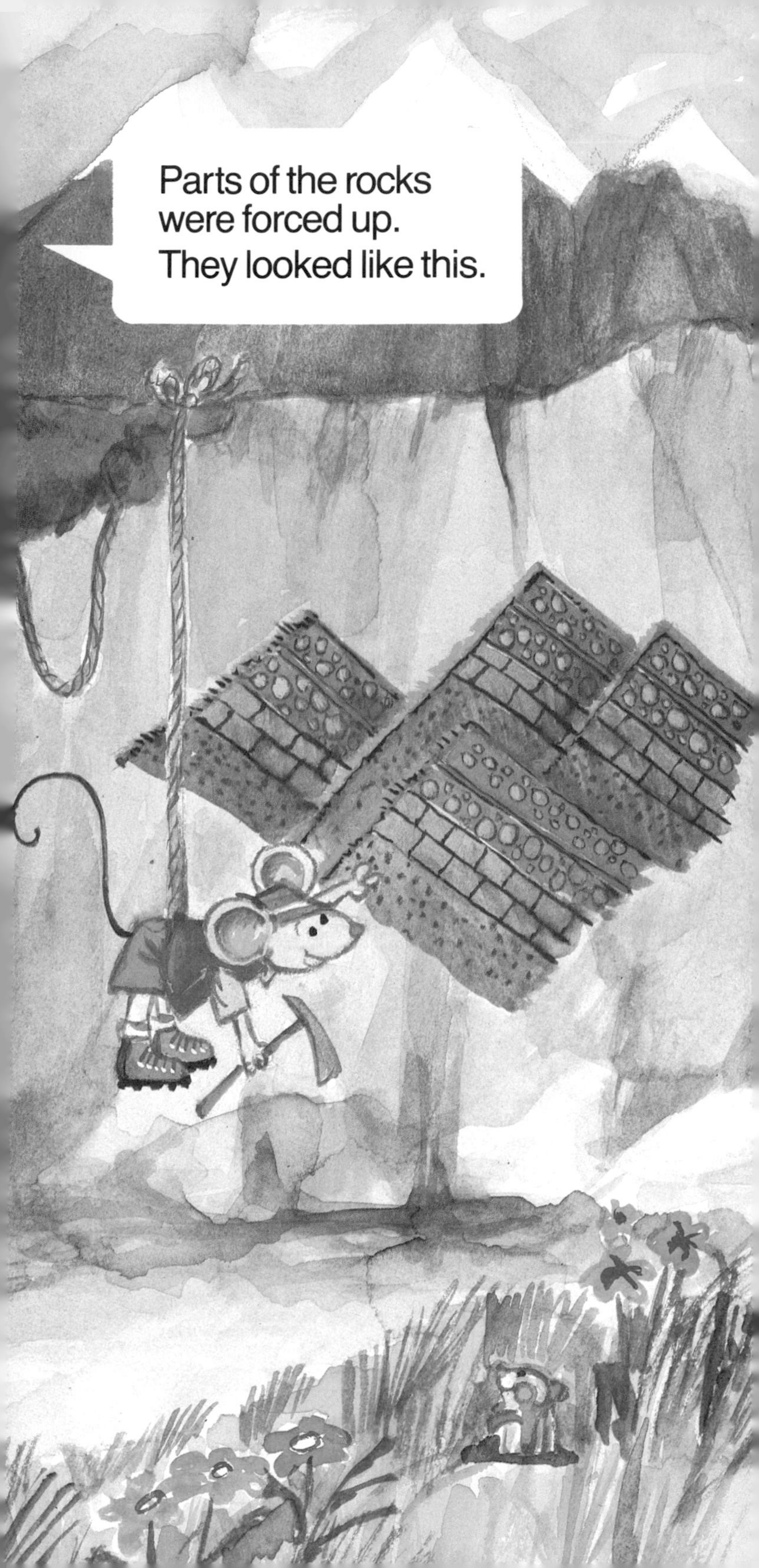
Parts of the rocks were forced up. They looked like this.

A third kind of mountain
was made by volcanoes.
The hot rock from the
volcano poured out.
It made layers and layers.

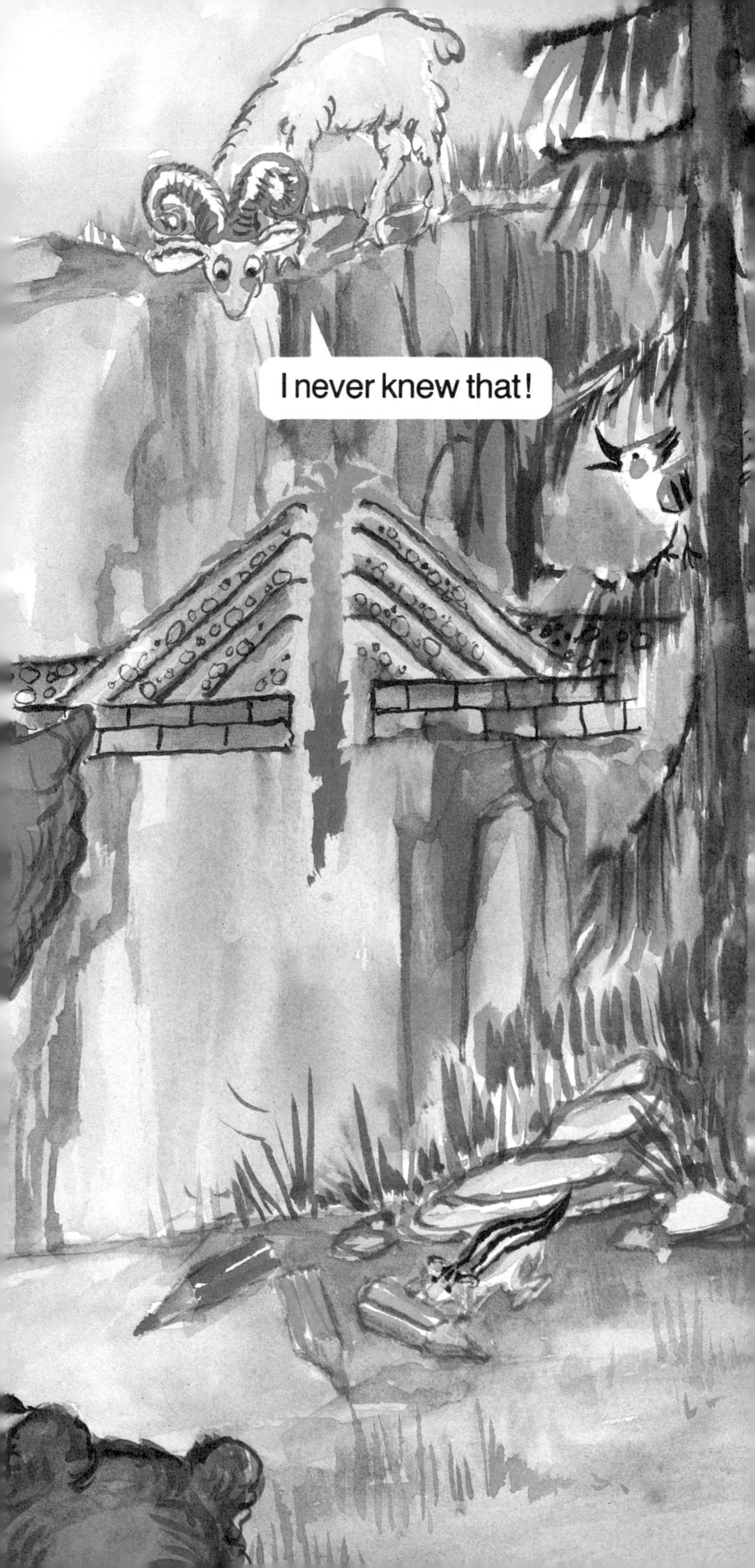
I never knew that!

Finally, many, many layers became a high mountain.

A fourth kind has a round top called a dome.
The rock layers were folded upward to make domed-shaped mountains.

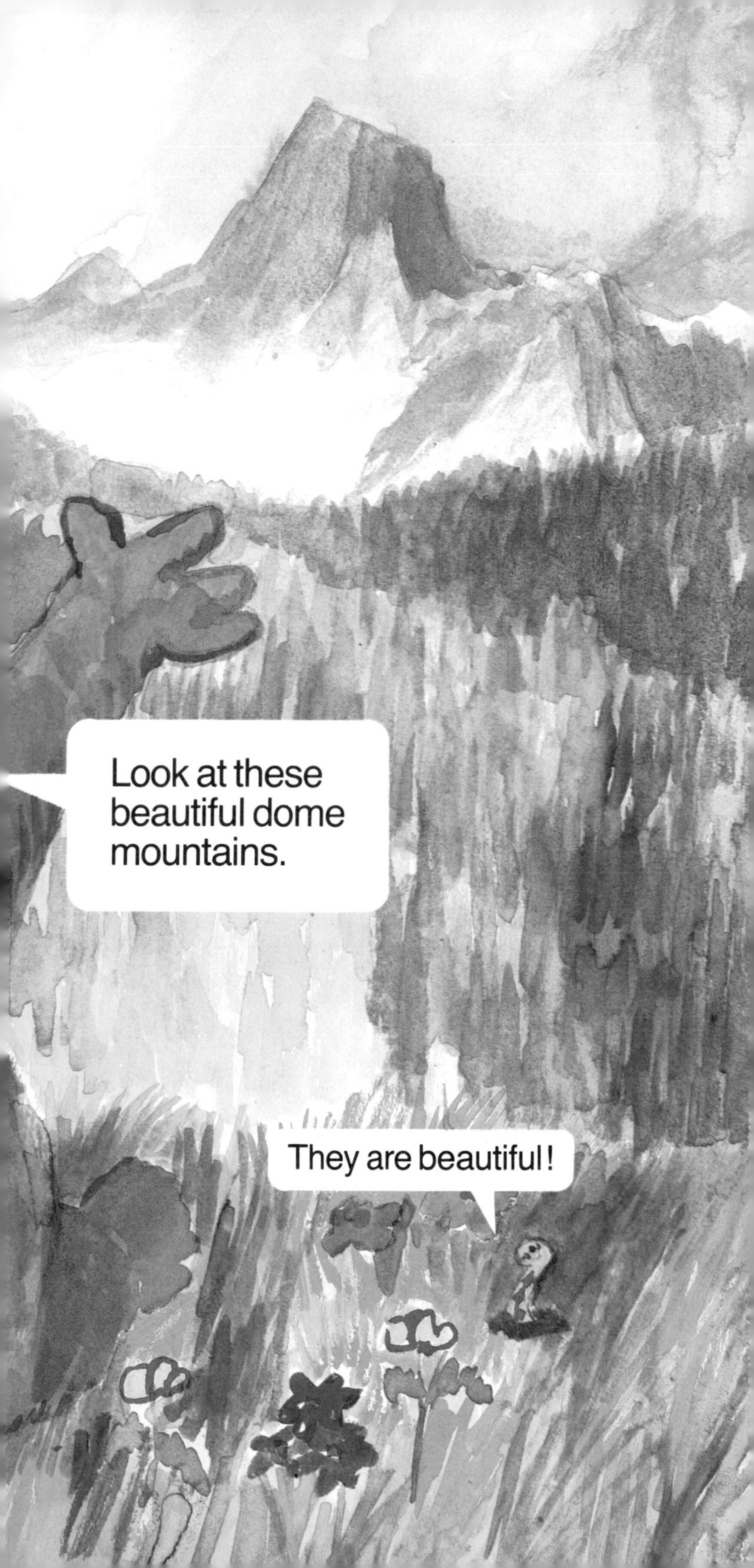
Look at these beautiful dome mountains.
They are beautiful!

Since mountains go high into the sky, it is very cool near the top.

It may be so cold that there is snow at the top all the time.

Plants and trees grow
on the mountain slopes.
At some high places,
it is so cold that
no plants grow.

There are many animals
in the mountains, too.

Mountain goats, sheep, deer,
moose, elk, and birds live
in the mountains.

Mountains are big and beautiful
homes for all these animals.

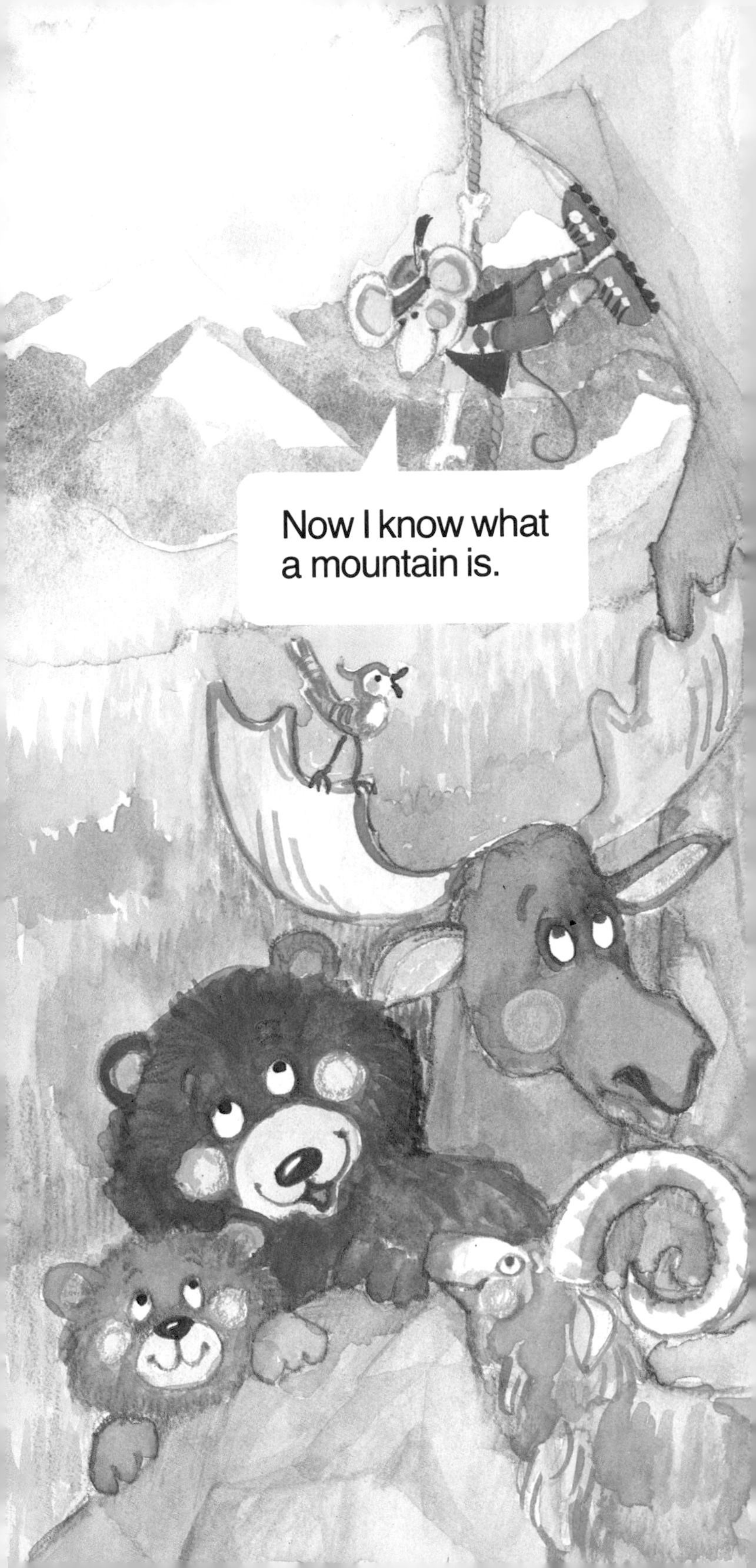
Now I know what a mountain is.